STUPENDOUS
Sports Stadiums

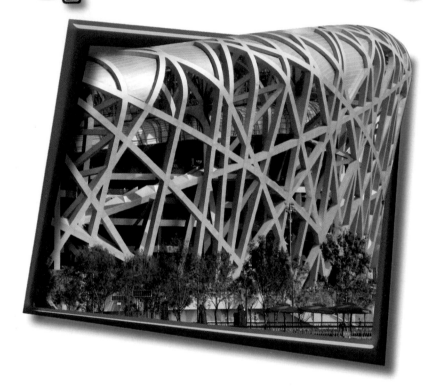

by Michael Sandler

Consultant: Paul F. Johnston, Ph.D.
Washington, D.C.

BEARPORT
PUBLISHING

New York, New York

Credits

Cover and Title Page, © sunxuejun/Shutterstock; TOC, © iofoto/Shutterstock; 4, © Ambient Images Inc./ SuperStock; 5, © Molly Riley/Reuters/Landov; 6, © Tom Fox/Dallas Morning News/Corbis; 7, © Scott Boehm/ Getty Images; 8, © sunxuejun/Shutterstock; 9, © iPhotos/Shutterstock; 10, © Kai Pfaffenbach/Reuters/ Landov; 11, © AP Photo/Ian Mainsbridge; 12, © Munshi Ahmed/Bloomberg/Getty Images; 13, © Susan Jefferies; 14, © Stuart Forster/Alamy; 15, © Westend61 GmbH/Fotofeeling/Alamy; 16, © Pichi Chuang/ Reuters/Landov; 17, © AFP/Getty Images/World Games/Newscom; 18, © Christian Petersen/Getty Images; 19, © Global Spectrum/Gene Lower/AZ Cardinals; 20–21, © Stefan Sonntag; 21, © AP Photo/Korea Pool via Yonhap; 22A, © AP Photo/Carlo Wrede; 22B, © View Pictures Ltd/SuperStock; 22C, © VenuesWest/The Western Australian Sports Centre Trust/Government of Western Australia; 22D, © Florian Kopp/imagebroker/Alamy.

Publisher: Kenn Goin
Senior Editor: Lisa Wiseman
Creative Director: Spencer Brinker
Photo Researcher: James O'Connor

Library of Congress Cataloging-in-Publication Data

Sandler, Michael, 1965–
   Stupendous sports stadiums / by Michael Sandler.
      p. cm.— (So big compared to what?)
   Includes bibliographical references and index.
   ISBN-13: 978-1-61772-302-5 (library binding)
   ISBN-10: 1-61772-302-9 (library binding)
   1. Stadiums—Juvenile literature. I. Title.
   NA6860.S26 2012
   725'.827—dc22
                              2011006637

For more information, write to Bearport Publishing Company, Inc.,
45 West 21st Street, Suite 3B, New York, New York 10010.
Printed in the United States of America in North Mankato, Minnesota.

070111
042711CGA

10 9 8 7 6 5 4 3 2 1

CONTENTS

Stupendous Sports Stadiums 4

Cowboys Stadium........................ 6

Beijing National Stadium 8

ANZ Stadium........................... 10

Marina Bay Floating Stadium 12

Allianz Arena........................... 14

World Games Stadium 16

University of Phoenix Stadium........... 18

Rungrado May Day Stadium 20

More Stupendous Sports Stadiums........... 22

Glossary................................... 23

Index 24

Bibliography 24

Read More.................................. 24

Learn More Online 24

About the Author........................... 24

STUPENDOUS SPORTS STADIUMS

Each year in the United States about 75 million people head to sports stadiums to watch Major League Baseball games. Another 20 million go to stadiums to see professional football games. Together, that number of people equals almost one third of the U.S. population. Big, big buildings are needed to accommodate these large crowds, and stadiums are built to hold them. Some seat 50,000, 75,000, or even more than 100,000 people.

The new Yankee Stadium was built in 2009, and seats about 50,000 people.

The best sports stadiums are more than just oval-shaped buildings that have rows of seats surrounding a playing field. Many have unique features that make them stand out from the rest. In this book, you will discover some of today's most stupendous sports stadiums—in America and all around the world.

Michigan Stadium in Ann Arbor, Michigan, is the largest football stadium in the United States. It holds nearly 110,000 people. A movie theater would need about 400 separate screening rooms to hold that many people.

COWBOYS STADIUM

Opened: 2009   **Where:** Arlington, Texas   **Seats:** 80,000–100,000 people
Stupendous Feature: Video display board

The Dallas Cowboys are the world's most famous pro football team. So it's only fitting that they play in the world's most famous football arena. Finished in 2009, the stadium cost about $1.2 billion to build. For that price, you could build about 5,000 average-size homes in the United States.

High-tech gadgets and oversize features are what make Cowboys Stadium unique. A mighty dome-shaped roof soars nearly 30 stories above the playing field. The roof is **retractable** with two giant panels that slide open in good weather and slide closed in bad weather. Building the roof took 14,100 tons (12,791 metric tons) of steel—that's enough steel to build 92 Boeing 777 jets.

To enter and exit, visitors can pass through giant glass doors at each end of the stadium. These doors are huge at 120 feet (37 m) high by 180 feet (55 m) wide—big enough for more than 20 school buses to drive through them at the same time!

Cowboys Stadium's **massive** video display board has four screens. The two screens facing the **sidelines** are the world's largest. Measuring 72 feet (22 m) high by 160 feet (49 m) wide, each one is as tall as a seven-story building and wider than three basketball courts.

The entire video display board weighs 600 tons (544 metric tons)—about as much as 120 African elephants.

The huge video display board hangs 90 feet (27 m) high in the air—so high that the White House could easily fit between the screens and the field.

BEIJING NATIONAL STADIUM

Opened: 2008   **Where:** Beijing, China   **Seats:** 80,000 people (91,000 originally)

Stupendous Feature: Bird's nest construction

The Olympic Games are the world's most important sporting event. When a country is chosen to host the games, it often constructs brand-new stadiums. For example, China built the Beijing National Stadium for the 2008 Summer Olympics. However, because of its unique construction, few call it by its real name. Most people just call it the "Bird's Nest."

A real bird's nest is made from a tangle of twigs and branches. To construct Beijing National Stadium, large square-shaped tubes were twisted around one another to create a nest-like shape. These hollow pieces of steel are incredibly long, as much as 984 feet (300 m) in length. A piece this long could wrap around the outside of a basketball court three times!

Building the stadium took 42,000 tons (38,101 metric tons) of steel. That's the same amount of weight as about 600 U.S. Army tanks.

If the Bird's Nest were unraveled, the steel tubes could stretch out for about 22 miles (35 km). That is almost double the length of the island of Manhattan.

Beijing National Stadium is the world's largest steel structure. It took thousands of workers to build—as many as 10,000 working at the same time.

ANZ STADIUM

Opened: 1999   **Where:** Sydney, Australia   **Seats:** 83,500 people (110,000 originally)
Stupendous Feature: Eco-friendly

ANZ Stadium was also built for the Olympics. At the 2000 Summer Olympic Games in Sydney, Australia, it earned fame for its massive size. At the time, it was the largest Olympic stadium ever built—with room for 110,000 fans.

ANZ Stadium is not only known for its size. It is also one of the most **eco-friendly** stadiums in the world. For example, many of the lights in the stadium are connected to **motion detectors**. If there are no people moving around, the lights automatically switch off.

ANZ's approach to garbage is equally eco-friendly. Sports fans at most stadiums create a lot of trash when they snack at games, but not at ANZ. Every single food item is sold in **recyclable** packaging. This means that each wrapper eventually gets reused instead of ending up in a **landfill**.

ANZ Stadium has about 112 miles (180 km) of electric cable to power signs, video displays, and elevators. Stretched out, this cable would be longer than the distance from New York City to Philadelphia.

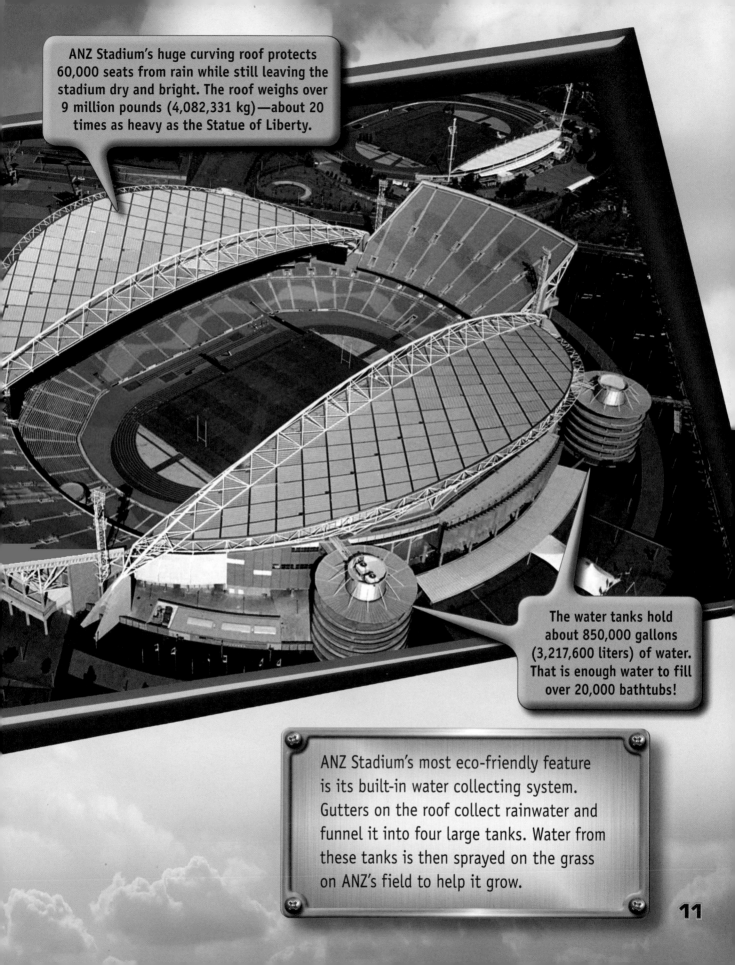

ANZ Stadium's huge curving roof protects 60,000 seats from rain while still leaving the stadium dry and bright. The roof weighs over 9 million pounds (4,082,331 kg)—about 20 times as heavy as the Statue of Liberty.

The water tanks hold about 850,000 gallons (3,217,600 liters) of water. That is enough water to fill over 20,000 bathtubs!

ANZ Stadium's most eco-friendly feature is its built-in water collecting system. Gutters on the roof collect rainwater and funnel it into four large tanks. Water from these tanks is then sprayed on the grass on ANZ's field to help it grow.

MARINA BAY FLOATING STADIUM

Opened: 2007 **Where:** Marina Bay, Singapore **Seats:** 25,000–30,000 people

Stupendous Feature: World's largest floating stadium

Singapore is the world's third most **densely** populated country. That means there are a lot of people living in a very small space. The crowded country has little room for big stadiums. So when Singapore needed a new one, a unique solution was found. The field portion of the stadium was built to float on the water in Singapore's **harbor** with only the **grandstand** built on land. Today, Marina Bay Floating Stadium is the largest floating stadium in the world.

The stadium's field is a giant platform on top of 15 floating **pontoons**. **Artificial turf** on top of the platform makes it perfect for playing soccer. The stadium can also be used for concerts, which makes it the world's largest floating stage, too.

With more than 18,000 people per square mile, Singapore is about 200 times more crowded than the United States.

A crowded street in Singapore

The stadium floats like a boat, but there's no danger of it sinking. The platform can support 1,179 tons (1,070 metric tons) of weight. That is the same amount of weight as about 300 fully loaded pickup trucks!

The platform measures 394 feet (120 m) long by 272 feet (83 m). That's big enough to fit nearly 500 bowling lanes.

ALLIANZ ARENA

Opened: 2005   **Where:** Munich, Germany   **Seats:** 69,900 people
Stupendous Feature: Unique air cushion exterior

In Munich, Germany, people see Allianz Arena long before they drive up to it. The stadium is hard to miss—it lights up the Munich night with its glowing, brilliant lights.

Two soccer teams call Allianz Arena home—FC Bayern München and TSV 1860 München. A fan can tell which one is playing just by looking at the stadium. For each game, the arena's lights match the color of the team that's playing: red for FC Bayern or blue for TSV 1860.

No other stadium in the world lights up like Allianz Arena because no other stadium has its unique **exterior**. Its outer surface is made of **translucent** plastic cushions that let light pass right through them. To give Allianz its incredible glow, 25,344 fluorescent tubes inside the stadium shine through the plastic.

The 2,760 plastic cushions on Allianz's exterior are made of incredibly thin plastic foil, just .007 inches (.02 cm) thick. That's less than half as thick as an ordinary kitchen trash bag. The foil sheets are sewn together and pumped up with air, much like party balloons.

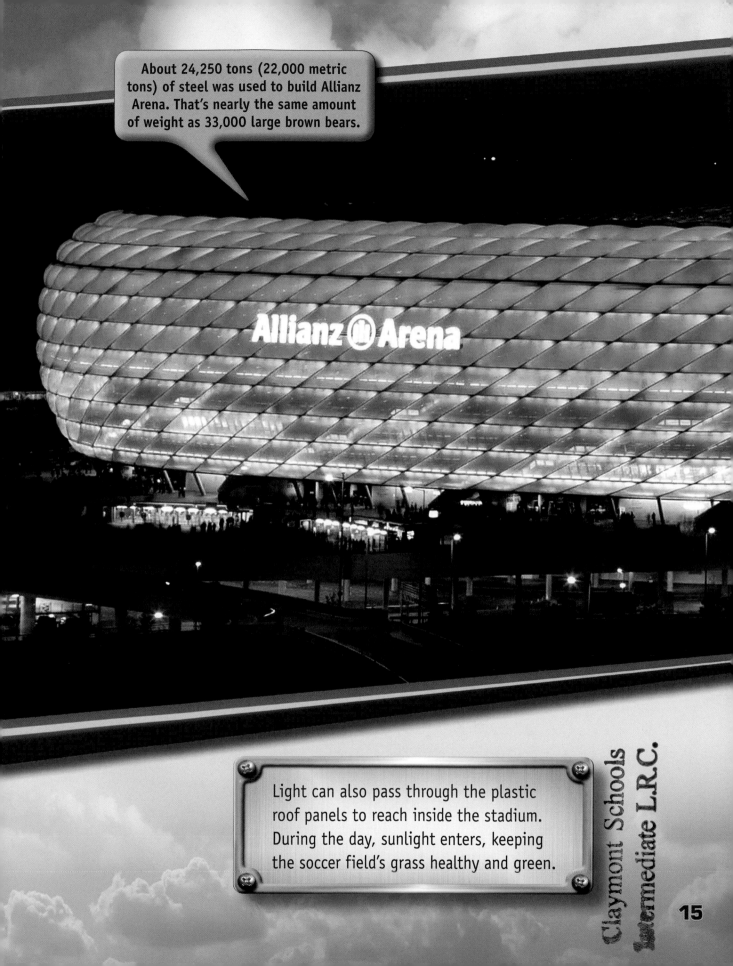

About 24,250 tons (22,000 metric tons) of steel was used to build Allianz Arena. That's nearly the same amount of weight as 33,000 large brown bears.

Light can also pass through the plastic roof panels to reach inside the stadium. During the day, sunlight enters, keeping the soccer field's grass healthy and green.

WORLD GAMES STADIUM

Opened: 2009   **Where:** Kaohsiung, Taiwan   **Seats:** more than 40,000 people

Stupendous Feature: World's largest solar-paneled stadium

Few stadiums are as stunning to see as World Games Stadium in Taiwan, which looks like a python ready to pounce. The stadium, however, is more than just incredible to look at. It's also extremely eco-friendly, built mostly from reusable materials. When the stadium is torn down decades from now, most of its parts and pieces won't end up in the trash. They will be reused instead.

The stadium's roof was also built with the environment in mind. It's covered with 8,884 **solar panels** that soak up the sun's rays and convert them to electricity. The panels power everything in the stadium from the lights to its two massive video screens to the elevators!

The World Games Stadium roof even produces electricity when the stadium is empty. This energy is used to power homes and businesses in the area.

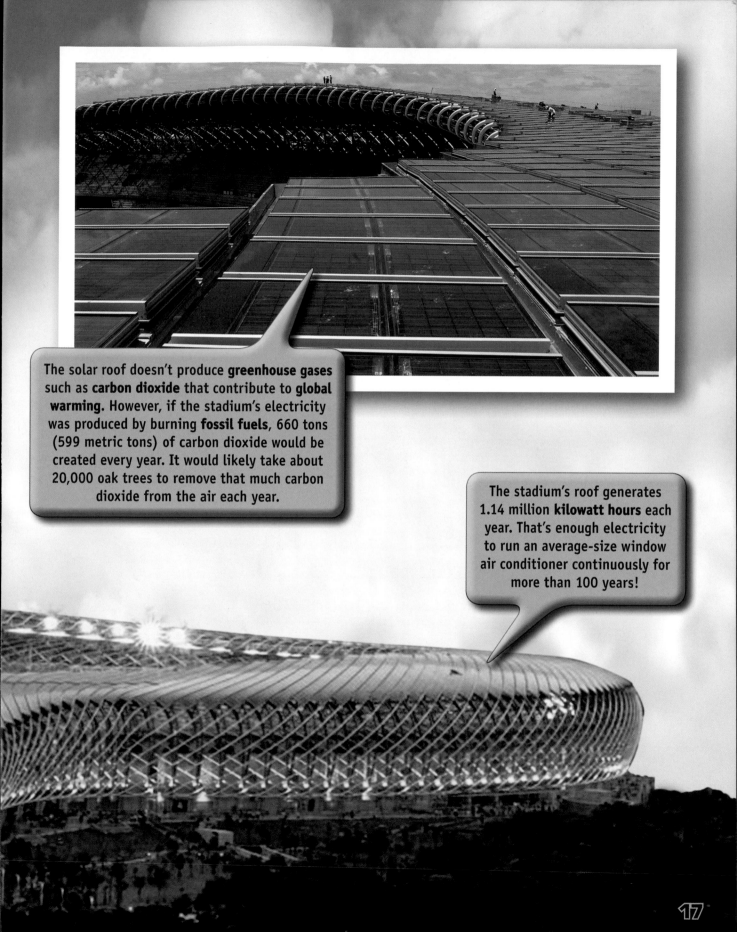

The solar roof doesn't produce **greenhouse gases** such as **carbon dioxide** that contribute to **global warming.** However, if the stadium's electricity was produced by burning **fossil fuels,** 660 tons (599 metric tons) of carbon dioxide would be created every year. It would likely take about 20,000 oak trees to remove that much carbon dioxide from the air each year.

The stadium's roof generates 1.14 million **kilowatt hours** each year. That's enough electricity to run an average-size window air conditioner continuously for more than 100 years!

UNIVERSITY OF PHOENIX STADIUM

Opened: 2006   **Where:** Glendale, Arizona   **Seats:** 72,200 people
Stupendous Feature: A fully movable grass field

For playing football, nothing beats a real grass field. NFL players love it because grass is softer than artificial turf, which means it's easier on their legs. Growing grass, however, is hard to do beneath a stadium roof. There's just not enough sunlight.

The **architects** of University of Phoenix Stadium, however, found a way to build a roof and give the Arizona Cardinals football team real grass to play on. The stadium floor—with the grass field on top—is a movable tray. It can slide right out of the stadium.

Most of the time, the field sits outside the stadium, where the grass can soak up the Arizona sunlight. On game days, the tray slides back inside on 13 train-track-like rails and more than 500 wheels.

The field inside the stadium on game day

The tray weighs an astounding 18.9 million pounds (8.6 million kg). That's about as heavy as 76 gigantic blue whales.

The movable grass field is truly massive at 403 feet (123 m) long by 234 feet (71 m) wide. That's more than 94,000 square feet (8,733 sq m) of green lawn—which could take about 10 hours to mow with an ordinary gas lawn mower.

RUNGRADO MAY DAY STADIUM

Opened: 1989   **Where:** Pyongyang, North Korea   **Seats:** 150,000 people
Stupendous Feature: Number of people it can hold

Stadiums are designed to allow many people to watch a game, concert, or other event at the same time. One stadium, Rungrado May Day Stadium in North Korea, does this job better than all the rest. With seating for 150,000 **spectators**, it's the biggest stadium in the world.

In fact, there can actually be more than 150,000 people inside the stadium. That's because May Day is often used for holiday shows that feature thousands of dancers, gymnasts, and other performers. These shows, called Mass Games, can include as many as 100,000 performers. Together along with the spectators, there can be more than 200,000 people in the stadium at once. That's about the same number of people that live in Tacoma, Washington, or Little Rock, Arkansas.

Yankee Stadium, with about 50,000 seats, would have to triple in size before it could hold as many people as May Day Stadium.

At Mass Games, thousands of people perform up in the stadium seats. The performers hold up different colored panels. When shown at the same time, they create massive pictures.

The massive pictures created by the performers are often called "the largest pictures in the world." They are about the size of two football fields!

MORE STUPENDOUS SPORTS STADIUMS

Maracana Stadium, Brazil

Though it holds far fewer people today, in 1950 Maracana Stadium held the largest stadium crowd in history for the final game of the **World Cup**—199,854 people. That's more than twice the number of people who have ever attended a World Series baseball game.

Braga Municipal Stadium, Portugal

Braga Municipal Stadium was carved right out of a rock **quarry**. Around 35 million cubic feet (991,089 cubic m) of granite were moved to build it. That is enough granite to fill about 400 Olympic-size swimming pools.

Challenge Stadium, Australia

Challenge Stadium uses **geothermal technology** to heat its swimming pools and showers. The heat comes from 2,625 feet (800 m) under the ground—over seven times deeper than the deepest subway station in the world.

Soccer City Stadium, South Africa

Rebuilt to host the first World Cup in Africa in 2010, this stadium was constructed using more than 8,598 tons (7,800 metric tons) of steel just for the roof. That's about the same weight as 1,900 really big hippopotamuses.

GLOSSARY

architects (AR-ki-tekts) people who design buildings and make sure they are built properly

artificial turf (ar-ti-FISH-uhl TURF) a grass-like playing field surface made from plastic or rubber material

carbon dioxide (KAR-buhn dye-OK-side) a greenhouse gas given off when fossil fuels are burned

densely (DENSS-lee) having very little space; crowded

eco-friendly (ee-koh-FREND-lee) something that's not harmful to Earth or the environment

exterior (ek-STIHR-ee-ur) the outside surface

fossil fuels (FOSS-uhl FYOO-uhlz) energy sources such as coal, oil, or natural gas made from the remains of plants and animals that died millions of years ago

geothermal technology (jee-oh-THUR-muhl tek-NOL-uh-jee) devices that use heat from deep beneath the Earth's surface to produce energy

global warming (GLOHB-uhl WORM-ing) the gradual heating up of Earth's air and water caused by a buildup of greenhouse gases, which trap heat from the sun in Earth's atmosphere

grandstand (GRAND-stand) the area of a stadium where the seats are located

greenhouse gases (GREEN-houss GAS-iz) carbon dioxide and other gases that trap warm air in the atmosphere so it cannot escape into space; the gases responsible for global warming

harbor (HAR-bur) an area of water where ships can safely stay or load and unload goods

high-tech (hye-TEK) the latest technology

kilowatt hours (KIL-uh-waht OURZ) a measure of electricity

landfill (LAND-fill) a large hole in the ground that serves as a dumping ground for garbage

massive (MASS-iv) giant, huge

motion detectors (MOH-shuhn di-TEK-turz) devices that can sense the movements of people, animals, or things such as trucks

pontoons (pon-TOONZ) floating structures that can be used to support things on water

quarry (KWOR-ee) an open pit from which stone or other material is dug up

recyclable (ree-SYEK-luh-buhl) able to be used again

retractable (ri-TRAKT-uh-buhl) able to be moved back and forth

sidelines (SIDE-lyenz) the lines that mark the longest sides of a football field

solar panels (SOH-lur PAN-uhlz) groups of solar cells that are connected to form flat boards or sheets that convert sunlight to energy

spectators (SPEK-tay-turz) people watching athletic contests, concerts, or other events

translucent (transs-LOO-suhnt) allowing some light to pass through

World Cup (WURLD KUHP) a global soccer tournament that takes place every four years

INDEX

Allianz Arena 14–15

ANZ Stadium 10–11

Arizona 18

Australia 10, 22

Beijing National Stadium 8–9

Braga Municipal Stadium 22

Brazil 22

Challenge Stadium 22

China 8

Cowboys Stadium 6–7

Germany 14

Maracana Stadium 22

Marina Bay Floating Stadium 12–13

Michigan Stadium 5

North Korea 20

Olympics 8, 10

Portugal 22

Rungrado May Day Stadium 20–21

Singapore 12

Soccer City Stadium 22

South Africa 22

Taiwan 16

Texas 6

University of Phoenix Stadium 18–19

World Games Stadium 16–17

Yankee Stadium 4, 20

BIBLIOGRAPHY

John, Geraint, Rod Sheard, and Ben Vickery. *Stadia: A Design and Development Guide.* Oxford: Elsevier (2007).

Architectural Record

Civil Engineering Magazine

www.stadia-magazine.com

READ MORE

Hurley, Michael. *The World's Most Amazing Stadiums.* Chicago: Raintree (2011).

Matthews, Sheelagh. *Beijing National Stadium.* New York: Weigl (2009).

Mitchell, Susan K. *The Largest Stadiums (Megastructures).* Pleasantville, NY: Gareth Stevens (2007).

LEARN MORE ONLINE

To learn more about stupendous sports stadiums, visit
www.bearportpublishing.com/SoBigComparedtoWhat

ABOUT THE AUTHOR

Brooklyn-based writer Michael Sandler has written numerous books for kids and teens.